MORE
SenseSational
Object Talks

by
Bonnie Bruno

STANDARD
PUBLISHING
Cincinnati, Ohio

The Standard Publishing Company, Cincinnati, Ohio. A division of Standex
International Corporation. © 1997 by The Standard Publishing Company. All rights
reserved. Printed in the United States of America.

04   03   02   01   00   99   98   97   5   4   3   2   1

ISBN 0-7847-0649-2

Cover design by Barry Ridge Graphic Design

Table of Contents

See for Yourself!

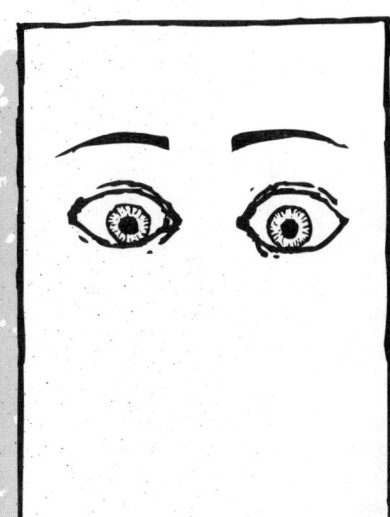

Just a Drop

God helps us say
"I'm sorry."

Materials needed
drinking glass, water, green food coloring

Scripture background
Colossians 3:12-14

Key verse
"Do not be angry with each other, but forgive each other. If someone does wrong to you, then forgive him. Forgive each other because the Lord forgave you" (Colossians 3:13).

Introductory questions

1. Is it sometimes hard to apologize?
2. How do you feel when your best friend makes a new friend?

The Talk

Jake and Nicholas were good buddies. Their moms were great friends, too.

"You boys have been friends since the playpen days," their moms would say.

But one day, Jake found a new friend. He met Cory at the playground. Cory was new in town, and lived just one block from Jake's house. Nicholas met Cory, and did not like him. "He's dumb," was all Nicholas would say. Then he told Jake that he would not play with him, as long as Cory was around.

Jake was crushed. "Why can't we all be friends?" he asked.

But Nicholas would not hear of it. .

(*Squeeze one drop of green food coloring into a glassful of water.*)

See what happens with just one drop? When we are jealous of someone, we can turn green with envy. That is what happened to Nicholas. He let jealousy cloud his friendship with Jake.

After a few days, Nicholas began to feel sad. He missed his

buddy. He wanted to say "I'm sorry," but the words would not come out.

Do you ever feel that way, too? Then you will be happy to know that God gave Nick the courage—finally—to apologize. And God will gladly do the same for you, if you just ask. (*Read key verse.*) God loves watching friends make up!

Shades of Blue

God appreciates our uniqueness.

Materials needed

pictures of a blue jay, cornflowers, and pictures that show several ethnic groups

Scripture background

Psalm 139:13-15

Key verse

"I praise you because I am fearfully and wonderfully made; your works are wonderful, I know that full well" (Psalm 139:14, NIV).

Introductory questions

1. What are some ways that you are one-of-a-kind?
2. Do you ever wish you were exactly like someone else? Explain your answer.

The Talk

Imagine what it must have been like on the day after the creation. Beautiful new sounds filled the air, trees rustled in a gentle breeze, and fresh, cool water flowed within reach.

Think about this: when God made the birds, he could have made thousands of the same kind. He could have made our feathered friends all the same shade of blue. Instead, he gave us blue jays (*show picture*), cardinals, and crows—each uniquely shaped and colored.

When God created flowers, he could have made them all blue like this cornflower (*show picture*), but instead gave us irises, tulips, and sunflowers. God must have had a wonderful time, creating our colorful world!

He could have made you and me the same, too. Instead, he planned for our world to be filled with a wonderful variety of people. (*Show pictures of different ethnic groups.*) He blessed us each with unique qualities, and helps us use them to the best of our abilities.

(*Read key verse.*) In this whole wide world, there is no one quite like you. Makes you feel pretty special, doesn't it?

What's in a Label?

God knows who we are inside.

Materials needed

two cans of fruit with switched labels, can opener

Scripture background

1 Thessalonians 5:13-18

Key verse

"Encourage the people who are afraid. Help those who are weak. Be patient with every person" (1 Thessalonians 5:14).

Introductory questions

(*Show the cans and read the labels to the children.*)

1. If you had to write a label for yourself, how would you word it?
2. Have you ever unfairly labeled someone by calling them a mean nickname?
3. Do you think God ever labels us?

The Talk

Robin loved crafts. Nothing went to waste when Robin was around. She could take scraps of paper, ribbon, and fabric, and make something beautiful. She even made her brother a birthday gift out of a recycled water jug.

"You're the most creative student I have seen in a long time," her teacher said.

One classmate did not agree, however. "You use too much glue, and the colors never match right," he told her.

Suddenly Robin didn't feel as creative anymore. She started thinking that her projects were too messy to give as gifts. Just a few words, spoken thoughtlessly, had the power to change the way Robin thought about herself.

Labels can either help or hurt. For instance, "kind-hearted" and "creative" are good labels. Calling someone "messy" or "clumsy" can be hurtful. (*Ask if students can think of more labels.*) Sometimes it's easy to put the wrong labels on people. (*Open the cans and show the contents.*) See how much confusion labels can cause? (*Read key verse.*) God wants us to help people and not to hurt them.

We can be glad, though, that God knows that the labels people put on us do not always tell the truth. He knows who we are, and wants to help us become all that he created and planned for us to be!

Even the Tiniest

God pays attention
to details.

Materials needed

small examples of creation, like a
feather, stone, wildflower, seashell

Scripture background

Matthew 6:25, 26

Key verse

"Look at the birds in the air.
They don't plant or harvest or
store food in barns. But your
heavenly Father feeds the birds.
And you know that you are
worth much more than the
birds" (Matthew 6:26).

Introductory questions

1. Do you like to take walks outside, especially in the woods? Tell
   me about something special that you have found outside on
   a walk.
2. Why do you think God made these? (*Show the objects you brought.*)

The Talk

A wooden birdhouse hung just outside a large living room window
at the Kummers's house. Every day from dawn until dusk, the
Kummers had a front-row seat. There they watched a pair of spar-
rows fly back and forth between a high backyard tree and the little
birdhouse. Carrying pieces of paper, string, straw, and pine needles,
the birds worked at preparing a fine nest.

And there they prepared for the arrival of their babies.

When the four eggs hatched, the Kummers watched as both
Mama and Papa Sparrow flew tirelessly in search of food. Back and
forth they worked until dusk, gathering and delivering nourish-
ment to their offspring.

But something disturbing was happening. One skinny little bird
seemed to be missing out! The bird in front grew strong and eager,
while the little one appeared to be wasting away, and the parents

did not seem to notice what was happening right before their very beaks!

But God noticed. One day, the bird in front had grown strong enough to leave the nest. When he flew away, the parents continued their dawn-to-dusk feedings.

One by one, the three remaining birds grew strong enough to fly away, also. God cares for the birds of the air. (*Read key verse.*) He watches over even the tiniest of creatures, and surely he watches over you and me, too!

Low Tide

God plants surprises in the least expected places.

Materials needed

"Surprise!" written on an index card and taped to underside of one student's chair; small treat for the one who discovers the card under her chair

Scripture background

Psalm 84:11, 12

Key verse

"The Lord God is like our sun and our shield. The Lord gives us kindness and glory. He does not hold back anything good from those whose life is innocent" (Psalm 84:11).

Introductory questions

1. Do you like surprises, or are you the type who would rather know exactly what will happen next?
2. Do you think God likes to surprise us?

(Ask them to look under their chairs. Give a small prize to the one who finds an index card with the word "Surprise!" written on it. Discuss the difference between a good surprise and a not-so-good surprise.)

The Talk

Megan was visiting the west coast for the very first time. While there, she visited an historic lighthouse, and later hiked to a nearby tide pool. Tide pools are areas bathed by the waves as they crash onshore. During low tide, marine biologists can study rocks and see what is living there in the warm pools of water.

Megan scrambled over huge rocks covered with springy mussels. The mussels clung to the rocks. Even the waves at night did not wash them away. Megan leaned down to study a pool of sun-warmed sea water. She touched a purple sea anemone, watched tiny crabs swimming by, and counted the orange starfish that lived on the lower sides of the rocks.

Low tide uncovers nature's surprises. *(Read key verse.)* Low tide shows us what a wonderful, creative God we have, a God who looks out for every living creature.

Sometimes our friendships can undergo a low period, too. And sometimes we discover surprises that are not that pleasant. Maybe we're surprised at how angry we can get, or how long we can stay mad. Or maybe we're surprised by a sour attitude in someone who always appeared so cheerful.

Let's be glad for low tides and the surprises they reveal. Why? Well, in nature they give us a chance to see more of God's beautifully crafted world. And in relationships they give us an opportunity to forgive those who hurt us and to make a good friendship even better!

Listen Closely!

Who Are You?

Our true identity comes from God.

Materials needed

various forms of identification (birth certificate, or driver's or marriage license)

Scripture background

Proverbs 3:1-4

Key verse

"Then you will be respected and pleasing to both God and men" (Proverbs 3:4).

(Show the various forms of identification. Ask the students if they can think of anymore.)

Introductory questions

1. How would you describe yourself to a blind person? (Remind them to include facets of personality, talents, and interests.)
2. What things do you like about yourself? What would you like to change?

The Talk

A ninety-year-old lady could no longer remember her name.

"Who are you, dear?" asked a new nurse who met her in the hall of the nursing home.

The old woman could only answer, "I'm George's wife." She could remember her life with George, but she had forgotten her own name!

When someone asks us who we are, we usually tell them our whole name, then we might add something like, "I'm Gary's son" or "I'm Lisa's neighbor." Who we are often depends on who we know or who our relatives are.

Who are you? (*Have the children whisper, and then shout, their own names.*) When you were shouting your own name, could you hear anyone else's? What about when you whispered? Sometimes you have to listen closely to find out who other people really are.

For those of us who trust Christ as Savior, our identity is brand new. We are children of God. Imagine that—a son or daughter of the living God!

(*Read key verse.*) When you act like the child of God that you are, people will respect you, because you will do what is right.

Words That Stick

God reminds us to speak kindly to one another.

Materials needed

assorted magnets, paper clips, tacks, and other small, metal objects

Scripture background

Psalm 19

Key verse

"I hope my words and thoughts please you. Lord, you are my Rock, the one who saves me" (Psalm 19:14).

Introductory questions

1. Have you ever said something that you wished you could take back?
2. Do you think God really cares how we speak to one another? Why does he care?

(*Pass out magnets and metal objects. Ask your students to experiment attracting the metal objects at different distances.*)

The Talk

Jared's little sister, Heather, wanted to do something nice for his birthday. But what? He had plenty of toys, and his bookcase was already overflowing onto his floor.

So she decided to *make* a present—something that he could not find in any store.

She gathered paper, markers, glue, and glitter. Mom let her spread newspapers on the kitchen table. There she worked most of the afternoon while Jared was visiting a friend.

When she finished, Heather had four beautiful book covers to wrap for Jared's birthday. One book cover had a drawing of dancing bears; the second, hopping frogs; the third, snapping turtles, and the fourth—well, the fourth was black.

"It's the night," she explained to Jared. "And the glitter is the stars."

Jared thanked Heather for her unique gift. Then he said five words that stuck with her rest of the day:

"They're just what I needed!"

Words stick, kind of like these metal objects do to magnets. Did you know that? Unkind words stick like pins, but kind words stick in hearts and minds, where happiness begins. (*Read key verse.*) Practice saying things that will please God. When we say loving things to people, we can often tell that they really click with that person, just like a paper clip "clicks" against the magnet. (*Demonstrate. Let them listen.*) Then we know we have done the right thing.

When was the last time you spoke happy, soothing words to someone special?

Like a Mighty Roar

God often speaks
to us when we stop
talking.

Materials needed

two tape recordings—one of silence (blank) and one of a lion's roar (check sound effects recordings at your local public library)

Scripture background

Proverbs 17:27, 28

Key verse

"A man of knowledge uses words with restraint, and a man of understanding is even-tempered" (Proverbs 17:27, NIV).

Introductory questions

1. Have you ever felt annoyed?
2. Are you more of a talker or a listener?

(Explain that you have brought two recordings. Ask them to listen, then describe what they have heard.)

The Talk

Silence. It is not often you encounter it, unless you are the only one awake in the middle night. And if you listen closely, you will discover that there are noises to be heard even then.

Wind batters window screens. Raindrops slap against the house. Clocks tick. Dogs bark. If someone at your house snores, you will definitely hear *that*!

Silence can be nice, or it can be uncomfortable. Some people don't feel good unless they are chattering all the time. They jump from topic to topic, like a butterfly on a bush. But did you know that even silence can be like a lion's roar?

(Read key verse.) Try this experiment. The next time someone says something annoying, practice keeping quiet. The next time you hear someone talking behind the back of a friend, don't join in. Silence

speaks louder than words!

Silence is also a time when we can draw closer to God. When you go home today, try praying with your eyes closed and thinking of God's goodness. Don't ask him for a single thing. Just thank him for loving you just as you are. Tell him what he means to you. Then sit silently and wait. You may be surprised at what he whispers to your heart!

Nothing to Say

God helps us to hear clearly.

Materials needed
cotton balls

Scripture background
Mark 7:31-37

Key verse
"They were really amazed. They said, 'Jesus does everything well. He makes the deaf hear! And those who can't talk—Jesus makes them able to speak' " (Mark 7:37).

Introductory questions

(Pass out two cotton balls per student. Ask them to use the cotton balls as ear plugs. Ask the following questions very quietly, so that they cannot hear you.)

1. Do you only listen carefully when something interests you?
2. How can we practice being better listeners?

(Ask them to remove the cotton balls. Repeat the questions and give them time to share their answers.)

The Talk

Have you ever gotten lost in a daydream? Maybe it happened in school, when you ought to have been paying attention to the lesson. It could have happened at home, when parents or siblings were speaking to you. They could not read your thoughts, so they probably figured that you just had nothing to say.

Sometimes it even happens in church, too. There you are, sitting in your usual spot with your friends or family. You sing along with everyone else, and you try to pay attention to the speaker, but somewhere along the way, your thoughts leave the room. They may not return until it is time to leave.

(*Read the key verse.*) Today's Bible verse talks about a person who could not speak clearly, because he was unable to hear. He was deaf. (*Ask how it felt to have cotton in their ears a few moments ago. Ask what it would be like to be deaf.*)

Jesus knew how much the man needed to hear and speak. So he traveled to the man's town, touched him gently, and made his ears hear and his lips speak.

How glad are you for ears that hear?

The next time you hear the voice of a family member, be glad! The next time you hear a bird sing, or a friend laugh, be thankful! And the next time you feel yourself slipping into a daydream during church, practice listening. You might be surprised at what God will teach you.

Smelly Stuff

Leave It to Max!

God buries our mistakes and never digs them up.

Materials needed

dog bone (or dog treat shaped like a bone), poster board, markers

Scripture background

Micah 7:18, 19

Key verse

"Lord, you will have mercy on us again. You will conquer our sins. You will throw away all our sins into the deepest sea" (Micah 7:19).

Introductory questions

1. How many of you have a dog?
2. Does your dog have a habit of digging?

The Talk

Max was a bundle of energy. Ever since he was a furry little pup, he liked to dig. He dug holes under the fence, holes in the flower bed, and even dug up vegetables in the garden!

"Max must be bored," Dad decided. "Let's give him a bone. Chewing is good for his gums and teeth." (*Show them the dog bone or treat.*)

But Max did not chew the bone. Leave it to silly Max—he dug a hole and buried it!

"Maybe we should rename him Digger," laughed Grandma.

Now, what do you suppose Max did the very next day? He sniffed the whole yard and he dug up the bone. You may ask, why bury a bone, only to sniff it out and dig it up? Doesn't make much sense, does it?

You and I dig every now and then, too. After we have made a mistake and said we're sorry, after we have asked God to forgive us, sometimes we take an invisible shovel and dig. Something reminds us of something bad we did—like the smell reminded Max of his bone—and we feel badly all over again.

Do you dig up your mistakes and let them bother you all over again? Do you waste time feeling guilty, once God has forgiven your sin?

Don't do that! (*Read key verse.*) Once God forgives us, he buries our sins in a deep hole. Then he hangs a sign that says (*use marker and poster to write out*) "No Sniffing and No Digging Allowed—Forever and Ever!"

Home

God never loses our address.

Materials needed
address book, stationery, scented stickers

Scripture background
Psalm 86:2-7

Key verse
"I call to you in times of trouble. You certainly will answer me" (Psalm 86:7).

Introductory questions

1. Has a friend of yours ever moved away? How did you feel when that happened?
2. Does your family have an address book? Whose addresses are is written in it?

The Talk

Kelly's friend, Chad, was moving to a city called Wakecliff. Wakecliff was a long way from the small town in Washington where they started school together.

"Don't worry," Chad said. "We can always write letters!"

He wrote his new address in a little blue book for Kelly. "I promise to write back," she told him.

Weeks passed, then months. Kelly wrote and Chad answered. Chad wrote and Kelly answered. Sometimes Chad would surprise Kelly with a scented sticker. (*Pass around scented stickers. Let the children smell them and let each child take one if you have enough.*) Once she even sent one that smelled like chocolate (*or whatever scent you have*). Mmm-mm!

Then the letters stopped.

"Has Chad lost my address?" wondered Kelly. "Has he forgotten me?" She found the stickers Chad had sent her, but they were getting old, and they didn't smell good anymore.

When was the last time you talked to God? Talking to God is like sending a wonderfully scented letter off to a friend. (*Read key verse.*) Sometimes you wait days or months (or even longer) for his answer. That's not because he doesn't care, but because the best answers take time. He does not forget you, and your prayers don't lose their scent like Kelly's stickers did.

God will never lose your address, either. Isn't that great news? And he doesn't even have an address book. God always knows exactly where to find you, because he is always watching over you. He will never move away. He will be there for you always!

Something in the Air

God is *always* near.

Materials needed
umbrella, raincoat

Scripture background
James 4:8-10

Key verse
"Come near to God, and God will come near to you" (James 4:8).

Introductory questions

1. Have you ever noticed how the sky changes right before a storm?
2. How do you feel after a storm passes, when the sun shines again?

(Use the umbrella and raincoat as props while you tell the story.)

The Talk

Ahh-hh. There's nothing quite like the smell of an approaching rain. Can you smell it? Sometimes, on a hot summer day, you will notice a wind beginning to blow. The temperature will cool several degrees in a short period of time. You might hear a thunderclap off in the distance.

But oh, that smell! The smell of rain in the air is a promise of refreshment. Even the hot, thirsty plants must bend their heads in anticipation.

To some folks, an approaching storm spells trouble. They concentrate more on the distant thunder than on the refreshing rain. It's almost as if they think the storm will last forever.

God has good news for us! (*Read key verse.*) Today's verse assures us that he is always near. He brings the rain, but he also sends the sun again afterwards.

If your life feels a bit stormy right now, you can be sure of this: God is right there in the middle of your storm. He knows what you are going through. He will see you through.

And before long, the sun will shine again.

Eau de Trash

God's way is always best!

Materials needed

trash can, disinfectant spray

Scripture background

1 John 3:14-19

Key verse

"My children, our love should not be only words and talk. Our love must be true love. And we should show that love by what we do" (1 John 3:18).

Introductory questions

1. What kinds of things end up in your trash can at home?
2. How can our words and actions tell others about God's love?

The Talk

Every night at 10:30 sharp, Earl can be found rummaging through the trash bin at Mel's Burgers. The place closes at 9:30. As soon as the employees leave, Earl climbs into the dirty trash bin.

You see, that is where Earl finds his next meal.

Earl has been living out of trash cans for over ten years. It has become a way of life. Some people tease him. His clothes are not clean. His hair is a mess, and his beard is scraggly. A group of kids nicknamed him "Eau de Trash," because he smells almost as strong as the trash bin.

But those same people have problems of their own. The cruelty they display leaves a terrible "odor" behind. Behavior like that shows a lack of love. It shows a lack of understanding of what others may be going through. (*Read key verse.*)

If you have a secret problem with making fun of others, here's what you can do. (*Spray the trash can with disinfectant. Make sure you are in a ventilated area and do not spray in the direction of the children.*) Tell God that you are sorry. Ask him to "disinfect" your heart and help you to think before you speak.

God loves helping us with our problems. And he loves it when we are honest enough to admit that his way is always best.

The Right Stuff

God supplies the strength to run from sin.

Materials needed

assorted shoes—baby shoes, thongs, high heels, heavy boots, and a pair of smelly sneakers; athletic equipment—weights, water bottle, etc.

Scripture background

Isaiah 40:28-31

Key verse

"The people who trust in the Lord will become strong again. They will be able to rise up as an eagle in the sky. They will run without needing to rest. They will walk without becoming tired" (Isaiah 40:31).

Introductory questions

1. Are you a fast runner?
2. Do you know what a marathon is? Have you ever heard of a baby running a marathon? (*Show each pair of shoes, except for the sneakers, pair by pair. Ask whether a person could win a race in each type of shoe.*)

The Talk

What kind of shoes do you run fastest in? How much of an athlete's success is talent, and how much of it is the type of shoe she is wearing? Does somebody wake up one morning and turn into an Olympic runner?

Of course not!

Years of training go into the making of any good athlete. Warm-up exercises, longer sprints, and finally, the run itself, help prepare the athlete who has her sight set on the goal ahead.

The Christian life is just like a race. How well you run depends on how well you train. Training takes practice. It takes patience. And it takes perseverance. (*Explain what "perseverance" means.*) When you exercise long and hard enough, you start to sweat. Spiritual perseverance is like working yourself into a spiritual sweat. (*Bring out smelly sneakers. Let them take a sniff if they want.*) The person who wore these sneakers did a lot of exercise in them, don't you think? (*Read key verse.*) How could you "exercise" spiritually?

Here's how. Practice every day by reading your Bible. You don't have to read a whole chapter. It is better to read a few verses and really think about them, than to rush through a whole chapter. Practice by talking to God. You don't need fancy words. You don't even have to be in a particular place. Just pray wherever you are. Some people even like to pray while they walk or rake the yard. God hears you wherever you are!

Practice, too, by treating others the way Jesus treated everyone he met. You can read all about Jesus in the New Testament. (*Show the New Testament in your Bible.*) Jesus was patient, forgiving, and kind to everyone he met.

Not sure how much training is enough? Don't worry. Just do it, and give the results to God.

Tasty

Until It's Stirred

God's Holy Spirit stirs our hearts.

Materials needed
glass of milk, chocolate powder or syrup, spoon, cups (optional)

Scripture background
1 Chronicles 16:8-12

Key verse
"Tell about all his wonderful things he has done" (1 Chronicles 16:9).

Introductory questions

1. What is a blessing?
2. Do you ever think about your blessings?
3. How do you think God feels when he hears us say, "Thank you"?

The Talk

(Pour a glassful of milk, add chocolate powder or syrup, and do NOT stir.)

Hmm-mm. This drink doesn't look much like the chocolate milk that I sometimes drink at home. Why not? (*Let them guess.*)

It needs stirring! Stirring blends the chocolate with the milk and makes it taste just right. (*Stir and taste.*)

Come to think of it, a lot of things in our world need a good stir before we use them. Some yogurts require stirring to get to the fruit at the bottom. House paint needs stirring. Frozen fruit juices and cake mixes need to be stirred.

You and I need an occasional stirring, too. Every now and then we need to remember what God has done for us. (*Read key verse.*) We need his Holy Spirit to "stir" us, to remind us of our many blessings. Blessings like the fact that he made each of us special! He loves us! He forgives us! He guides us! He wants the best for us! He provides food, clothing, and shelter for us every day!

(*Tell them that you would like to share a time of "stirring." Ask for volunteers to say one-sentence prayers of thanks to God. If you would like, have enough pre-made chocolate milk for everyone to have some.*)

Not Clean Enough

God says that we are "clean" when we ask him to forgive us.

Materials needed

pictures of germs, as seen under a microscope (check your library), magnifying glass

Scripture background

Isaiah 1:16-18

Key verse

"The Lord says, 'Come, we will talk these things over. Your sins are red like deep red cloth. But they can be white as snow. Your sins are bright red. But you can be white like wool' " (Isaiah 1:18).

Introductory questions

1. How clean are your fingernails today?
2. Do you know what germs look like under a microscope?

The Talk

(*Show microscopic pictures. Then ask for volunteers who would be willing to look at their fingernails through a magnifying glass.*)

Alyssa loved summer camp. She filled her days with softball, hiking, and helping build a lean-to shelter for her sleep-out under the stars.

But one afternoon, Alyssa lost track of time. When she heard the dinner bell ring, she tossed her hammer and raced down the hill toward the dining hall.

33

"You barely made it in time, young lady," said Mr. Strickland. Mr. Strickland was the one who stood at the door checking hands for cleanliness.

"Hmm," he said with a grin, "Looks like you've been working on that lean-to again."

Alyssa was really hungry. Her mouth was watering and she wanted to run in and grab some dinner. "I washed them," lied Alyssa, then added under her breath, "this morning."

"Hurry and wash. Dinner will wait for you," said Mr. Strickland.

Alyssa was so hungry for food that she lied about her hands being clean enough. Sometimes things like being hungry can make us do and say things we shouldn't. (*Read key verse.*) Have you ever thought about the price that Jesus paid to wash away our sins? He gave his life for you and me. It is as if all the sins of the world were piled on his shoulders. Because of Jesus, God declares all who believe in him "clean." He will never say, "Sorry, you're not clean enough!" Jesus scrubbed away the stain of our sins, now and forever.

So Many Details

God's Word gives us the perfect recipe for happiness.

Materials needed

Bible, tomato products (ketchup, sauce, puree, paste, juice)

Scripture background

Psalm 16:7-11

Key verse

"You will teach me God's way to live. Being with you will fill me with joy. At your right hand I will find pleasure forever" (Psalm 16:11).

Introductory questions

1. Have you ever made up your own recipe?
2. Why is it important to include every ingredient in a recipe?

The Talk

(Show the assortment of tomato products and explain that although they are different, they sprang from the same source—tomatoes. Open the jars and let the children taste the difference if you, and they, wish.)

Ricky wanted to do something special for his mother. "I will cook dinner on Tuesday," he told her excitedly. "When you get home, it will be ready to eat!"

"Sounds great," agreed Mom. "And if you need help, Dad will be close by."

Ricky found his favorite recipe in Mom's little wooden box—spaghetti sauce! He checked to be sure that he had all the necessary ingredients: ground beef, onion, garlic, tomato sauce, tomato paste, and Italian seasoning.

"Uh-oh," he mumbled to himself. "There isn't any tomato paste."

Ricky checked the cabinet one more time. "This will work," he said, grabbing a red-labeled can.

Ricky cooked the meat, then added all the remaining ingredients. But when he tasted his sauce, he almost choked. The sauce had a peculiar flavor. It was so spicy, his tongue hurt and his eyes watered!

Ricky checked the trash can. "Mexican tomatoes," read the red-labeled can. He used hot and spicy Mexican tomatoes!

"I guess I just read the 'tomatoes' part," he told his dad.

Dad laughed. "Hey, it could have been worse. You could have added that can of pineapple!"

Later, he told Mom, "Recipes sure have a lot of details."

(Read key verse. Hold up Bible.)

God's Word is detailed, too. In fact, at times it seems almost like a recipe. It teaches us all the right ingredients for living a godly life. It shows us how to get along with others, and how to please God. The Bible teaches us love in action. And just like the spaghetti sauce recipe, God's recipe for life is best when shared!

The Taste of Defeat

Victory is sweet, but a humble heart is even sweeter.

Materials needed
sponge, water

Scripture background
Jeremiah 9:23-24

Key verse
"This is what the Lord says: 'Wise men must not brag about their wisdom. Strong men must not brag about their strength. Rich men must not brag about their money' " (Jeremiah 9:23).

Introductory questions

1. How does it feel when you hear a winner bragging about his or her win?
2. Have you ever felt big-headed?

The Talk

Joey and Craig entered a school poster contest. The winning poster would be printed, and businesses all over town would display it in their front windows.

Joey was a great artist. He painted detailed scenes about the importance of practicing good safety. Craig, on the other hand, was a super writer. His poster featured a clever poem about safety.

Forty-three students entered the contest. A rally was held to announce the winner.

Joel and Craig both held their breath when Mr. Ketchum stood up. "This was a tough decision," he told the hushed crowd. "The posters are all creative, but we had to choose a winner, and the winner is. . ."

Craig jumped to his feet and was halfway there, before waiting for the rest of Mr. Ketchum's announcement: ". . . Joey Martin!"

Joey leapt from his chair and ran to the front. Proudly he

accepted the prize—a new set of 36 markers.

(*Ask students to gather around. Place dry sponge in water.*) Here is what happened as Joey's head began to swell with pride. But for Craig, the taste of victory was much too brief. He shuffled back to his seat, in time to hear Joey's voice booming through the gym speakers, "My poster is the best! I knew I'd win!" All of the sudden Craig went from feeling like he was eating his favorite ice cream to having a big plate of lima beans in front of him.

Do you know someone like Joey? Maybe each of us has a little bit of Joey in us. Maybe the joy of winning makes us forget for a minute about how others are feeling. (*Read key verse.*)

Let's ask God to give us a humble heart—a heart that helps us treat everyone like a winner!

Name That Pickle!

God's answers comes only when the time is right.

Materials needed

packet of cucumber seeds, cucumber, jar of pickles

Scripture background

Psalm 40:1-2

Key verse

"I waited patiently for the Lord. He turned to me and heard my cry" (Psalm 40:1).

Introductory questions

1. What does "patience" mean?
2. When are you impatient?

The Talk

Grandma could hardly stand the excitement! Her garden was ready for harvesting. By Friday she would have enough cucumbers to make homemade pickles.

"Try this old family recipe," said her friend, Bernice. "I'm sure you'll love these dills."

Grandma worked for six hours on Friday, stuffing cucumber slices into quart-sized jars. At the end of the day, twenty jars of dills sat on her counter.

"Grandma, can I please have a pickle?" asked five-year-old Angie.

"No, honey," answered Grandma. "We have to wait overnight for the spices to settle in."

The next morning, Angie brought a jar of pickles to Grandma. "Are they ready yet?" she asked.

Grandma opened the jar. "Okay," she said. "The first pickle goes to Angie!"

One bite was all it took.

"Ohh-hhh!" cried Angie, and ran to the garbage with a mouthful of pickle.

After she had spit it out, she blurted, "It tastes all vinegary! What do you call these pickles, Grandma?"

Disappointed, Grandma threw out every last pickle. That afternoon she returned the recipe to Bernice. "I'm sure I must have done something wrong," Grandma sighed.

"Oh no!" gasped Bernice. "You threw them out? Oh, what a shame!"

She went on to explain. "I usually wait six to seven weeks before tasting a pickle. You have to be very patient if you want good dills."

Sometimes when we pray, we get frustrated when God does not give us what we want. Impatiently we ask, and impatiently we wait for his answers. We want, we want, we want—and we want it right now.

(*Read key verse.*) God does hear us. And he does answer— when the time is right. If we grab for things at the wrong time, they may be bitter and unpleasant, like Grandma's pickles. (*Pass out the pickles if you wish.*) God's timing is perfect.

Handle With Care!

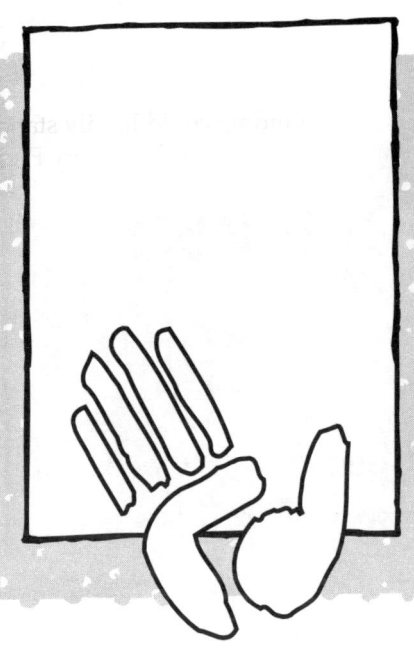

Splinters and Splints

God hugs us when we are hurt.

Materials needed

splint, tweezers

Scripture background

Colossians 1:10-12

Key verse

"God will strengthen you with his own great power. And you will not give up when troubles come, but you will be patient" (Colossians 1:11).

Introductory questions

1. What are some of the reasons why you run?
2. Why do some people always seem to be in a hurry?
3. Do you think God is ever in a hurry?

The Talk

Road blocks. Long lines of people. Detours. Signs that read "Closed for Lunch," "Closed for Repair," "Closed to Winter Traffic," "Closed for the Holiday."

Some things just slow us down, don't they? Picnics have to be postponed. Appointments must be canceled. And once in a while we have to stop everything because of a painful injury.

There's only so much we can do at times like that. If it's a splinter, we can use these. (*Show tweezers*). Perhaps it's a serious injury that requires a splint. (*Show splint.*)

We hurt. We mumble and grumble and may even ask, "Why me, Lord?"

But did you know that God can use even splinters and splints to teach us something important? When we have to stop everything and slow down, God can teach us patience.

(*Read key verse.*) Patience is a gift that will help us all through our lives. Patience helps us slow down and think about what is most important. One day we will look back and remember how God helped us by slowing us down long enough to allow him to hug away our hurt.

What If?

God uses our hands for good.

Materials needed

enough sturdy cutouts of a hand pattern for each child, either pre-made or made by the children; hole-punch; yarn

Scripture background

1 Thessalonians 4:9-12

Key verse

"Make it your ambition to lead a quiet life, to mind your own business and to work with your hands" (1 Thessalonians 4:11, NIV).

Introductory questions

1. Think about your hands for a moment. How important are they?
2. Name some good your hands can do.

The Talk

Two hands. Ten fingers.

With our hands, we can grip, shake, pull, push, pick up, put down, pat, or polish. (*Ask kids to think of other things you can do with your hands.*)

Margaret's hands are 93 years old. Gnarled and swollen, they ache with arthritis. She cannot do all that she used to do. But every day she sits in her chair by the window and folds her hands in prayer. Every day Margaret prays for everyone she knows, and even many whom she does not know.

Richie's hands are small. He is only five years old. His hands help carry groceries from the car into the kitchen. They pick up toys and put away books.

Kaitlin's hands are busy. She works at a fast-food restaurant. Her hands wrap hamburgers and fill cups with cold drinks. Kaitlin serves the public with her hands.

Mr. Wright's hands lie in his lap, stilled by a car accident. He cannot lift or grip, or work with his hands anymore. He misses his hands. Sometimes he dreams that he is building beautiful cabinets like he used to.

(*Read key verse.*) What if we all used our hands to help others? What if we all prayed like Margaret? What if we all did our share, like Richie and Kaitlin? And what if we all offered to lend a hand—our hand—to help someone like Mr. Wright, who can no longer use his own hands? (*Pass out hand cutouts. Punch a hole in the top and tie yarn through it, or let the children do that themselves.*)

Write your name on this hand. Hang it in your room as a reminder. Every day ask God, "What would you like my hands to do today?"

Hold That Thought!

God's love corrects us gently.

Materials needed
two-foot length of rope

Scripture background
Deuteronomy 8:2-6

Key verse
"He took away your pride. He tested you. He wanted to know what was in your heart. He wanted to know if you would obey his commands" (Deuteronomy 8:3).

Introductory questions

1. How well do you follow directions?
2. When someone refuses to listen to your warning, then gets into trouble, are you ever tempted to say, "I told you that would happen!"?

The Talk

Life is filled with consequences. If you choose to behave a certain way, you will get certain results. If you treat others kindly, you will usually receive the same kindness in return. If you are mean to others, they may be mean to you.

God gives us instructions. The instructions are right there in our Bible, for us to read and memorize.

Live at peace. Love one another. Forgive those who hate you. Avoid quarrels. Be honest in everything you do.

Ignoring God's instructions will bring consequences. (*Ask if they understand this term.*) Ignoring God's Word is like laughing at him and saying, "I don't believe you. I want to do things MY way."

(*Show them the two-foot length of rope. Put it on the table where all can see.*)

Try pushing this rope. (*Wait for all who want a turn.*)

43

Pretty impossible, isn't it? Too often, we push against the advice of people who know better than us. It might be a teacher, or your parents, or even God. We try to do things our way instead of listening.

(*Read key verse.*) God is a loving Father. He lets us stumble at times, then picks us up, dusts us off, and gently asks, "Why didn't you listen, my child?"

Hold that thought! Maybe it will help the next time you are tempted to do things your way.

The Only Way to Rake

God gives us the right tools to get the job done.

Materials needed
hoe, broom, rake

Scripture background
Philippians 4:8, 9

Key verse
"Continue to think about the things that are good and worthy of praise. Think about the things that are true and honorable and right and pure and beautiful and respected" (Philippians 4:8).

Introductory questions

1. What are some of the tools you or your mom and dad use in the yard? What are they used for?
2. What does "substitute" mean?

The Talk

It was a warm Saturday morning.

"Son, I'd like you to rake the yard before you play," Dad said.

Mark searched for the rake, but it wasn't in the garage. Instead of walking to the backyard shed, he lazily grabbed the nearest substitute. (*Show the hoe.*) But hoes are not made for raking!

Mark trudged back to the garage to get a different yard tool. (*Show the broom.*) But when he tried to sweep the leaves, they just sat there like wet paper. The broom was a poor substitute for a rake.

Dad peeked out the front door. "How is it going, son?" he called.

"Not very well," replied Mark.

He heard Dad chuckle. "Well, maybe you need this. I found it in the backyard." (*Show rake.*)

Sheepishly, Mark took the rake from Dad. "Thanks."

The right tool made all the difference. Mark was finished in fifteen minutes flat.

Think about it. Would you trim a hedge with scissors? Would you mow the lawn with a butter knife? Would you water the garden with a teaspoon? Of course not! To do the job right, you need to have the right kind of tool.

(*Read key verse.*) This verse from the Bible helps us think about the right kinds of things. The Bible is a different kind of tool. It is a spiritual tool. A spiritual tool helps us to draw closer to God. Prayer is another kind of spiritual tool, and so is going to church.

We can always talk *about* God, instead of to him. We can always read books *about* God, instead of his book, the Bible. We can even tell others *about* God, without knowing him personally.

But there are no substitutes for an active relationship with our Creator! And when we invite him into our lives, he provides the exact tools we need for living as Christians.

Are you using God's tools yet?

One Plain Lump

God is our Potter!

Materials needed

picture of a potter at work, lump of clay

Scripture background

Isaiah 29:15, 16

Key verse

"You are confused. You think the clay is equal to the potter. You think that an object can tell the person who made it, 'You didn't make me.' This is like a pot telling its maker, 'You don't know anything' " (Isaiah 29:16).

Introductory questions

1. Have any of you seen a potter at work? If so, what do you remember most about it?
2. Is there anything that God does not know about? Explain your answer.

The Talk

(*Show the picture of the potter. As you tell the following story, begin softening and shaping your lump of clay. Make it into a heart.*)

Zach wanted to go to his friend Bradley's house. His parents would be gone until 7:00 P.M. and they could do anything that they wanted.

"We can watch a movie and make popcorn," Bradley told him.

Zach asked his parents if it would be okay.

"Where does Bradley live, son?" asked Dad.

"Oh, not too far away," said Zach. "A friend of his big brother is going to drive us home from school."

"Do you have his address or his phone number?" wondered Mom.

"Um . . . I don't know," answered Zach.

Mom and Dad exchanged that certain *look*. Zach knew what was coming next.

"Why don't you ask Bradley if he can come here instead," they suggested.

Zach's face fell. He ran to his room.

The next day at school he told Bradley that he could not visit his house when his parents were not home.

"Then you could come to my house today," whispered Bradley. "We could get a ride home at lunch time when my brother and his friend go there."

Bradley leaned in closer and whispered, "And my brother could even write a permission note for you. Your teacher would think it was from your mom!"

Zach thought about it for a few minutes. "It would only be for a little while," he figured. He could come right back to school after lunch. Mom and Dad would never know! But then it would be like lying—both to them and to his teacher.

Each of us has to make some tough decisions sometimes. It's not easy saying "no" to a friend. Sometimes it's easier to think, as Zach did, that your parents will never know. If you were Zach, what would you do?

(*Read key verse. Show them the heart you made from the clay.*)

See this heart? It represents the heart that God gave me. God is my potter. He shaped me into someone special. He made me exactly like he wanted me to be, and he knows what I should do. I am his creation—who could know better than he does what is good for me?

He also gave me a heart to follow him. He gave you a heart that wants to love and obey him, too. When you choose to obey your parents, you are also choosing to obey God, the potter, who commanded us to listen to what our parents say.

Obeying your parents is the perfect way to say, "Thank you," to the one who gave us life!